Migratory and wintering shorebird monitoring at Cape Hatteras National Seashore, 2006-2007

Natural Resource Technical Report NPS/SECN/NRTR—2009/189

Michael W. Byrne, and Jessica M. Maxfield
Southeast Coast Inventory and Monitoring Network
Cumberland Island National Seashore
PO Box 806
Saint Marys, GA 31558

Joe DeVivo
Southeast Coast Inventory and Monitoring Network
National Park Service
100 Alabama St., SW
Atlanta, GA 30303

March 2009

U.S. Department of the Interior
National Park Service
Natural Resource Program Center
Fort Collins, Colorado

The Natural Resource Publication series addresses natural resource topics that are of interest and applicability to a broad readership in the National Park Service and to others in the management of natural resources, including the scientific community, the public, and the NPS conservation and environmental constituencies. Manuscripts are peer-reviewed to ensure that the information is scientifically credible, technically accurate, appropriately written for the intended audience, and is designed and published in a professional manner.

The Natural Resources Technical Reports series is used to disseminate the peer-reviewed results of scientific studies in the physical, biological, and social sciences for both the advancement of science and the achievement of the National Park Service's mission. The reports provide contributors with a forum for displaying comprehensive data that are often deleted from journals because of page limitations. Current examples of such reports include the results of research that addresses natural resource management issues; natural resource inventory and monitoring activities; resource assessment reports; scientific literature reviews; and peer reviewed proceedings of technical workshops, conferences, or symposia.

Views, statements, findings, conclusions, recommendations and data in this report are solely those of the author(s) and do not necessarily reflect views and policies of the U.S. Department of the Interior, NPS. Mention of trade names or commercial products does not constitute endorsement or recommendation for use by the National Park Service.

Printed copies of reports in these series may be produced in a limited quantity and they are only available as long as the supply lasts. This report is also available from the Natural Resource Publications Management website (http://www.nature.nps.gov/publications/NRPM) on the Internet.

Please cite this publication as:

NPS D-240, March 2009

Contents

Introduction

Overview

Cape Hatteras National Seashore (CAHA) serves several vital functions in shorebird conservation; it provides breeding habitat, important stop-over areas for migrating birds, and wintering habitat for a variety of species. Shorebirds are key components of coastal ecosystems and a primary reason for visitation by many visitors. Several species of special conservation concern use CAHA for some part of the year, including piping plover (*Charadrius melodus*), red knot (*Calidris canutus*), American oystercatcher (*Haematopus palliates*), and Wilson's plover (*Charadrius wilsonia*). These four species were the focus of 2006/2007 shorebird-monitoring efforts and henceforth collectively referred to as "focal shorebirds."

Piping plover use a variety of habitats during the migratory period and in winter for foraging (e.g., wash zone, intertidal ocean beach, wrack lines, washover passes, mud, sand and algal flats, and shorelines of streams, ephemeral ponds) (Loegering 1992, Hoopes 1994), however these habitats must be available and free from disturbance (Lafferty 2001).

North Carolina is currently the only state on the Atlantic Coast that has piping plovers during all phases of the annual cycle (Cohen 2005). Band sightings indicate that plovers from all three North American breeding populations use CAHA during migration and the winter, including plovers from the endangered Great Lakes population (Cohen 2005). In November, 2008, U.S. Fish and Wildlife Service designated approximately 2,043 acres of critical habitat within CAHA, Pea Island National Wildlife Refuge (contained within the boundaries of CAHA) and adjacent State lands. Approximately 1,827 acres of the designated critical habitat are contained within lands managed by CAHA (Federal Register 2008).

Between 2000 and 2005, the highest number of nonbreeding plovers at CAHA occurred during fall migration, which begins in July and peaks between August and September. Fall counts were highest at South Ocracoke, followed by Oregon Inlet (Bodie Island Spit, Pea Island National Wildlife Refuge, and formerly Green Island which is now largely unusable due to vegetation growth), then Hatteras Spit and Cape Point (Figure 1). Fall migration may last until November.

According to Cohen (2005), the first banded winter residents may appear in July, however, the majority of wintering birds arrive in August. The nonbreeding population from Dec. – Jan. likely consists entirely of winter residents. Cohen (2005) surmised that the wintering population of piping plover was possibly 20-35 birds. And based on that assumption Cohen et al. (2008) estimated wintering population size at Oregon Inlet only to be about 11 birds. Cohen (2005) noted the highest single counts of piping plover from 2000-2005 data occurred at Oregon Inlet and Ocracoke Inlet. It is difficult to assess the variance around these numbers because the study did not include error estimates resulting from detectibility or double-counting of individuals.

Spring migrants may appear in February or early March, and their numbers peak in late March or April (Cohen 2005). Sites at Oregon Inlet have had the highest abundance of spring migrants, followed by Ocracoke Inlet, with fewer numbers at Hatteras Spit and Cape Point. Ecological factors governing the distribution and size of the nonbreeding population at CAHA are unknown.

The red knot undergoes one of the longest migrations of any bird; from their nesting grounds in the northern Arctic to their wintering grounds in southern Chile, stopping at CAHA during the duration of the migratory period (Harrington 2001). Birds with long migrations are more dependent upon adequate habitat than birds that undertake shorter migrations (Piersma and Baker 2000). They tend to be gregarious as migrants, thus increasing the likelihood of local-scale disturbances (e.g., hunting, disease, harassment) having a more substantial impact of the migrating flock. Population abundance is estimated to have decreased 30% since 1980 (Donaldson et al. 2000).

Data suggest American oystercatcher abundance is declining throughout the southeast (Davis et al. 2001). The U.S. Shorebird Conservation Plan lists American oystercatcher as a species of extreme high priority (Brown et al. 2001). The effects of human-induced disturbance on American oystercatcher remain unknown (Davis et al. 2001). The largest American oystercatcher wintering populations occur in Virginia, North Carolina, and South Carolina (Nol and Humphrey 1994); however, information regarding migratory and wintering habitat use is limited (Meyers 2005).

Wilson's Plover do not winter at CAHA, but migrate through CAHA from breeding grounds in Maryland and Virginia during the spring and fall. The U.S. Shorebird Conservation Plan lists Wilson's Plover as a species of high concern (Brown et al. 2001). Harrington et al. (1989) estimated fewer than 1,000 birds comprise the Atlantic coast population.

The following analysis is the result of first-year (pilot) implementation of the long-term shorebird monitoring protocol developed by Byrne et al. (2009). Results of this study served as a means for protocol refinement; including modification to the sampling design and observation-specific data collected.

Justification for Study

- Migratory and wintering piping plover at CAHA consist of the threatened Atlantic Coast population and the endangered Great Lakes and northern Great Plains populations; which are protected under the Endangered Species Act of 1973 (as amended in 1982). Consistently and systematically collected data on trends in presence, timing, and habitat use for this species, however, do not exist for CAHA.

- The Recovery Plans for all three piping plover populations highlight the limited current knowledge on migratory and wintering patterns and emphasize the need for more information (USFWS 1988, USFWS 1996, USFWS 2003).

- The aforementioned shorebirds are likely good indicators of beach/ dune ecosystem condition as they are sensitive to habitat perturbations.

- This presents an opportunity for across-governmental agency and non-governmental organization cooperation and data-sharing as shorebirds migrate and winter across many jurisdictional boundaries and are systematically monitored in many locations (e.g., CACO, Great Lakes)

- The National Parks Omnibus Act of 1998 includes a congressional mandate for Parks to provide information on the long-term trends in the condition of their natural resources.

- Data are limited regarding frequency of habitat use by the aforementioned shorebirds and relative abundance of wintering populations.

- Terms and Conditions of the 14 August 2006 Biological Opinion state "The NPS must monitor presence, abundance, and behavior of migrating and wintering piping plovers from August 1 to March 31 of each year. Specific observations should be made relative to the above parameters with respect to the level and types of human activity in the area".

Methods

Study Area

Cape Hatteras National Seashore is part of the east coast barrier island system (Figure 1). The Seashore consists of 14,326 ha of land and 121 km of beach. The U.S. Fish and Wildlife Service administers Pea Island National Wildlife Refuge within the boundary of the Seashore. The Seashore has recently been designated a Globally Important Bird Area by the American Bird Conservancy because of the importance of the Seashore's habitats to avian breeding, migration, and wintering. Developmental pressures inside and outside the Park, potential modification of geomorphic processes resulting from Hwy 12 and the associated artificial dune, predation, and recreational uses represent the major categories of threat to the integrity of natural resources at CAHA. As is the case in all National Seashores in the Southeast, adjacent property development has resulted in direct loss and fragmentation of habitat upon which numerous park wildlife species were partially dependent. Other threats to natural resources include off-road vehicle use, the introduction of non-native plants and animals, and dredging of channels adjacent to the park.

Definitions of the term "habitat type" follow that proposed by Daubenmire (1968), despite the fact these communities are disturbed to such an extent that, in general, successional processes occur on a limited scale. See Table 1 for descriptions of the shorebird habitat types used in this study and Figure 6 for a conceptual representation of habitat type juxtaposition.

Sampling Design

The population of interest in this protocol are focal shorebirds that migrate through or winter at CAHA. All accessible ocean- and sound-side coastal areas at CAHA deemed as potential focal shorebird migratory or wintering habitat were included in the initial sampling design, and are defined as the sampling frame. The sampling units used for this protocol were the park miles. At the outset of protocol development and implementation, there were 62 park miles at CAHA. To facilitate consistency among wildlife programs at CAHA, the sampling areas chosen as the sampling unit of this protocol are based on the Sea Turtle Management Zones. These units are roughly one-mile segments of beachfront established by the North Carolina Wildlife Resources Commission statewide, and several segments have been designated as sampling locations for the Program for Regional and International Shorebird Monitoring (PRISM) / International Shorebird Survey (ISS) protocol. A shared, or similar, sampling unit among the sea turtle- and shorebird-monitoring programs may further increase the utility of these data in assisting with management decisions and contributing to larger-scale monitoring efforts.

The sampling regime for this protocol consisted of a two-tiered sampling approach that called for sampling shorebirds at a combination of high- and low-intensity sampling units. The high-intensity units were located in were accreted areas in the Park (i.e., spits / points) and the low-intensity units were all other oceanside / beachfront areas. Allocation of sampling units (i.e., park miles) into one of the two respective sampling regimes was the result of suspected, anecdotal, and previously observed focal-shorebird use. High intensity areas in CAHA included five sites: Bodie Island Spit, Hatteras Island Cape Point, Hatteras Island Spit, Northeast Ocracoke Island, and Ocracoke Island Spit. The Park was divided into four sub-units for shorebird monitoring to reduce sampling inefficiencies due to long travel times between sampling sites: Bodie, South Hatteras, Middle Hatteras, and Ocracoke (Figures 2-5) (Byrne et al. 2009). Each sub-unit has an approximately equal number of sampling units.

Table 1.
Shorebird habitat types at Cape Hatteras National Seashore (Bloom 1998, Hoffman and Shroyer 2004, Komar 1998, Leatherman 1979, York, L., Coastal Geomorphologist, SER, NPS, pers. comm.).

Habitat Type	Habitat Type Description
Backdune	The dune farthest from the beach
Backshore	Beach zone landward of the berm crest and the normal high-tide line; this zone is subject to wave action only during storm or extreme high tide conditions
Blowout	A flat or bowl-shaped area in the primary dune line where dune sand has been eroded away by wind; the bowl in this area may accumulate water or be eroded to the water table
Foreshore	The intertidal area that lies seaward of the berm crest
Inland freshwater pond	Freshwater wetland resource with $\geq$ 50% open water
Inland freshwater wetland	Freshwater wetland resource with < 50% open water
Intradunal swale	Low-lying areas between primary dune and backdune; may have wetland / wetland fringe vegetation of short hydroperiod
Mud flat / Algal flat	Area of minimal wave action and exposed at low tide; predominantly devoid of vegetation; substrate typically composed of sand, silt, and clay; areas occasionally have thin algal layer; commonly located between barrier islands and mainland; can have moderate to large amounts if organic material in sand
Overwash	A breach in the primary dune line resulting from swash uprush during storms or extreme high tides; often produces a fan-like feature as sand is deposited inland beyond the dune system(s)
Primary dune	The dune closest to the beach; land feature formed from an accumulation of windblown sand; these features are often covered with vegetation
Salt marsh / Tidal creek / Brackish Marsh	Area dominated by non-woody, halophytic plant species and tidally influenced
Sand flat	Accretion zone from downdrift of offshore sediment transport with minimal vegetative cover and slight elevation above sea level (e.g., a spit); occasionally has ponded water; exposed at low tide; has little or no organic material in sand
Secondary dune, tertiary dune, etc.	Dune between primary dune and backdune, increasing with distance from beach; land feature formed from an accumulation of windblown sand; these features are often covered with vegetation
Surf zone / Open water	Area immediately seaward of the foreshore
Wrack line	Beach zone where marine debris (natural and artificial) is deposited; often indicates high-tide line

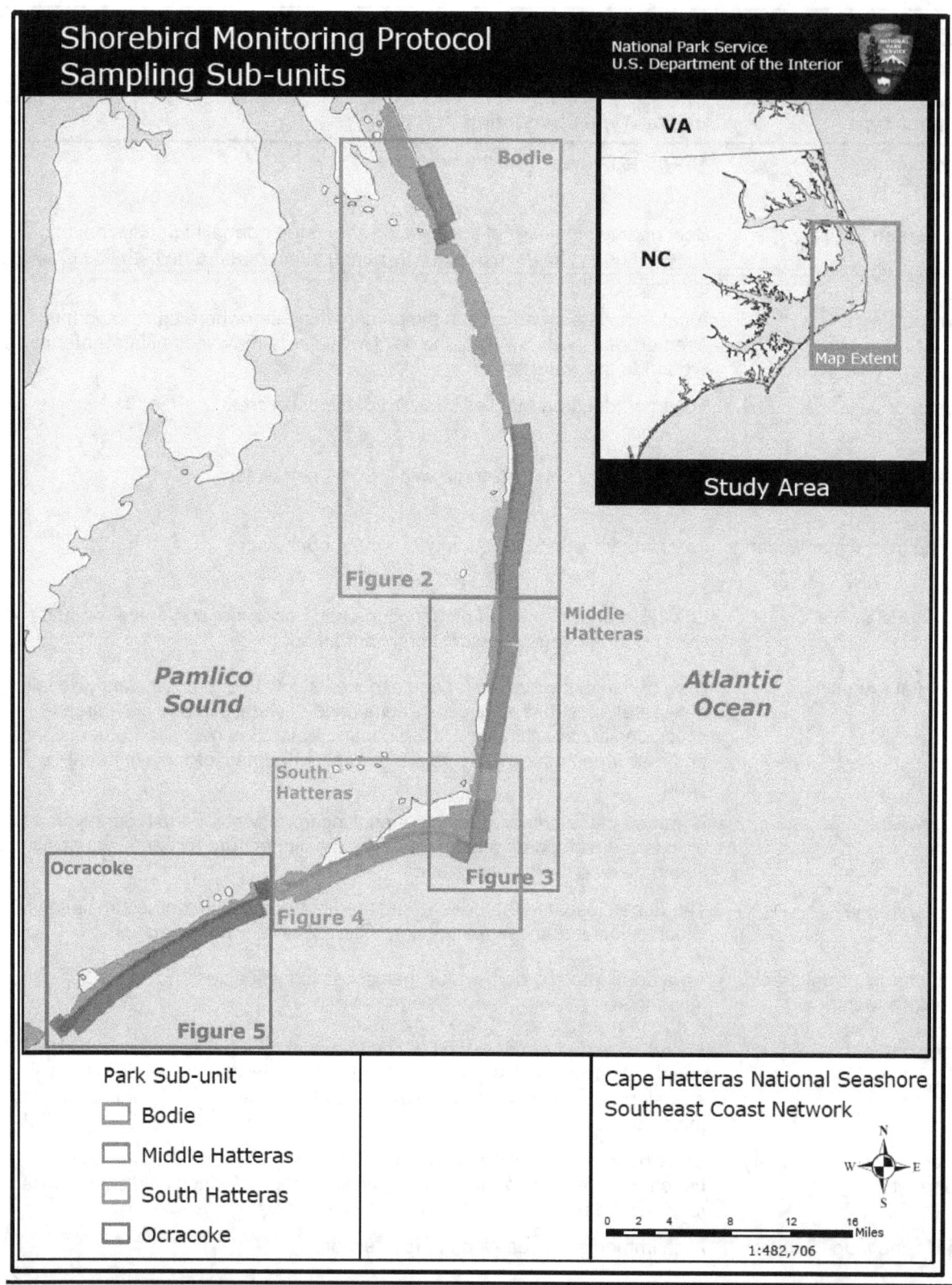

Figure 1. Geographic location of Cape Hatteras National Seashore, the four sub-units identified in this protocol, and the park miles used as sampling units.

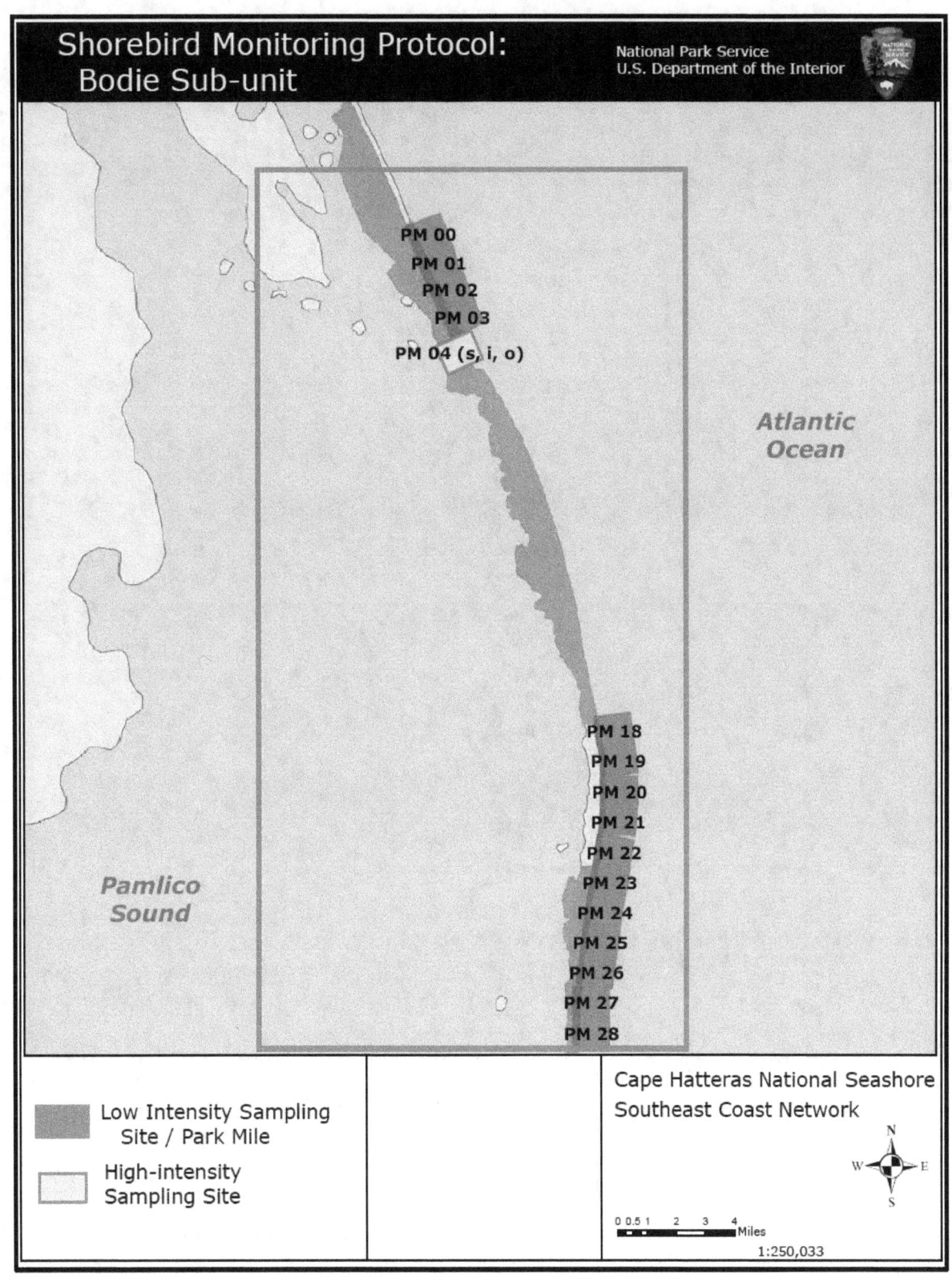

Figure 2. Bodie sub-unit at Cape Hatteras National Seashore. [PM – Park Mile].

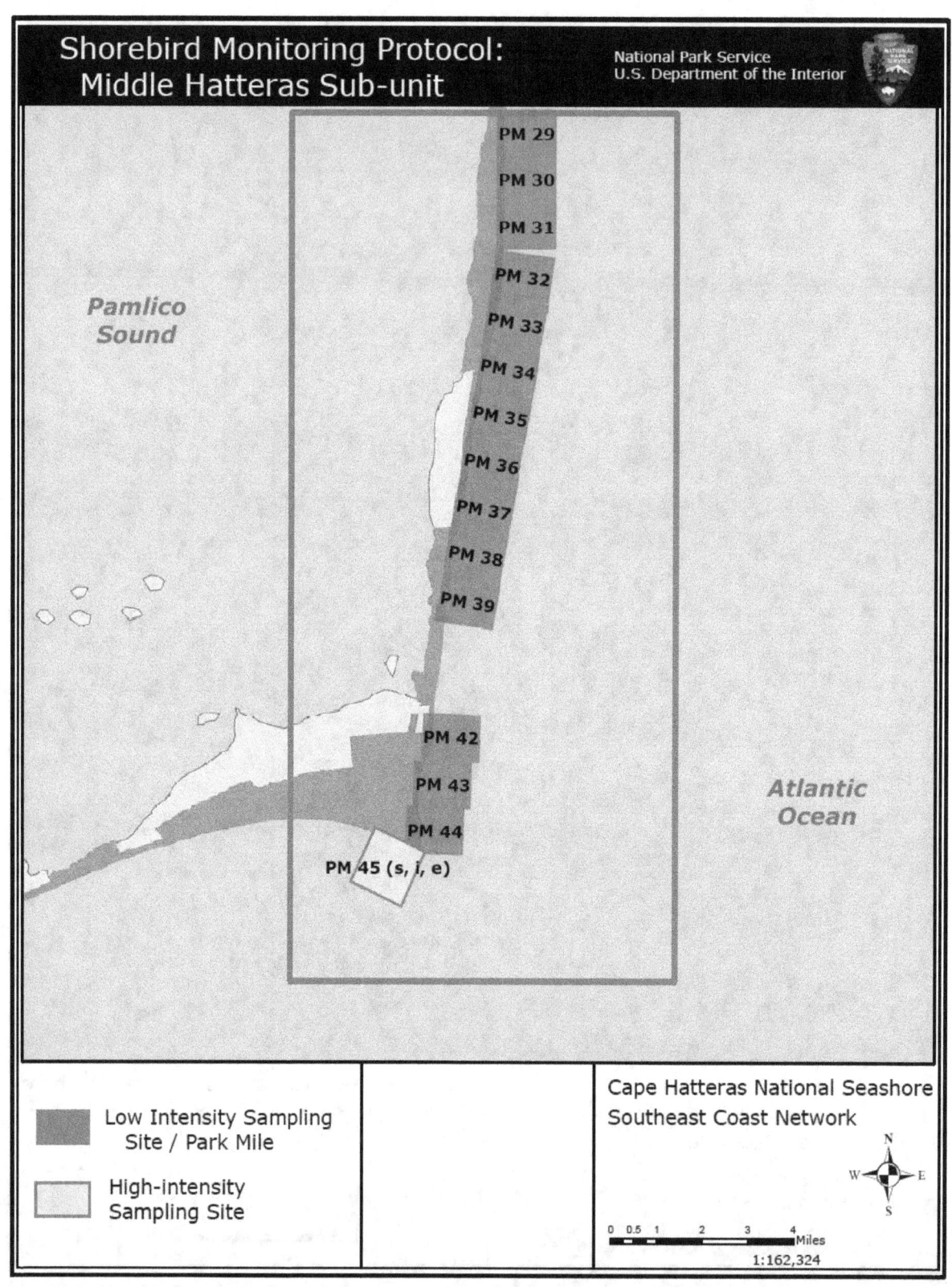

Figure 3. Middle Hatteras sub-unit at Cape Hatteras National Seashore. [PM – Park Mile].

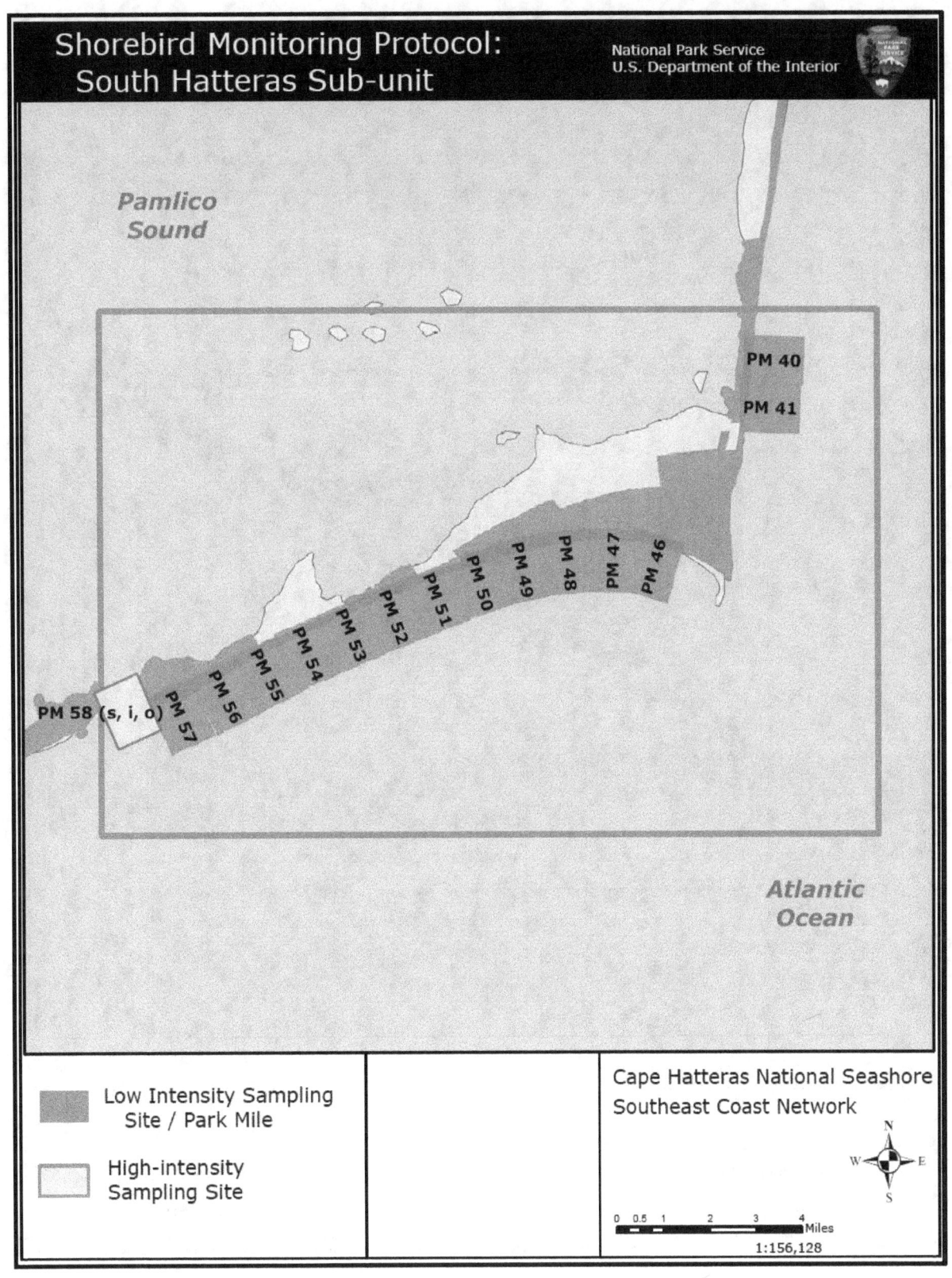

Figure 4. South Hatteras sub-unit at Cape Hatteras National Seashore. [PM – Park Mile].

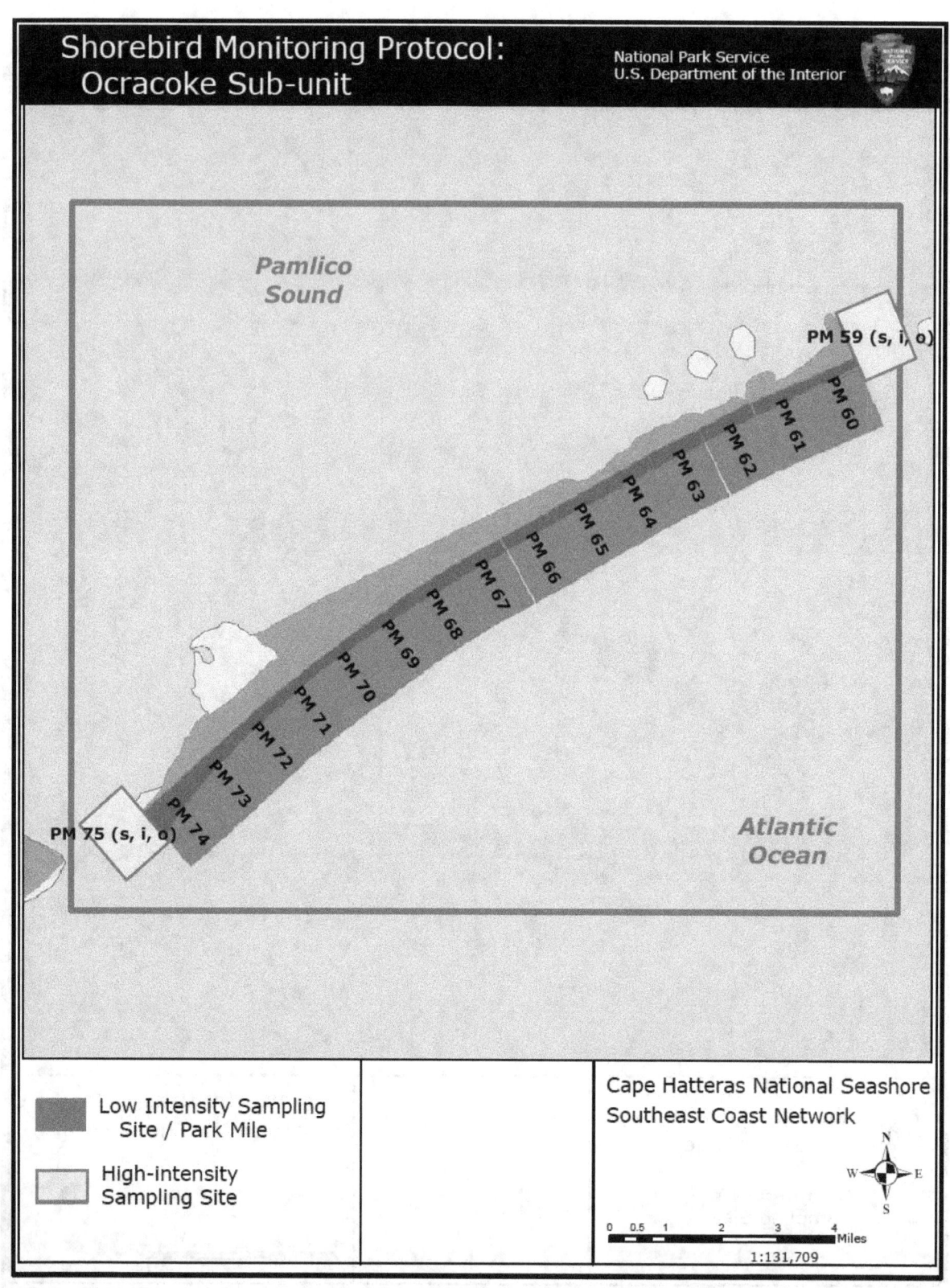

Figure 5. Ocracoke sub-unit at Cape Hatteras National Seashore. [PM – Park Mile].

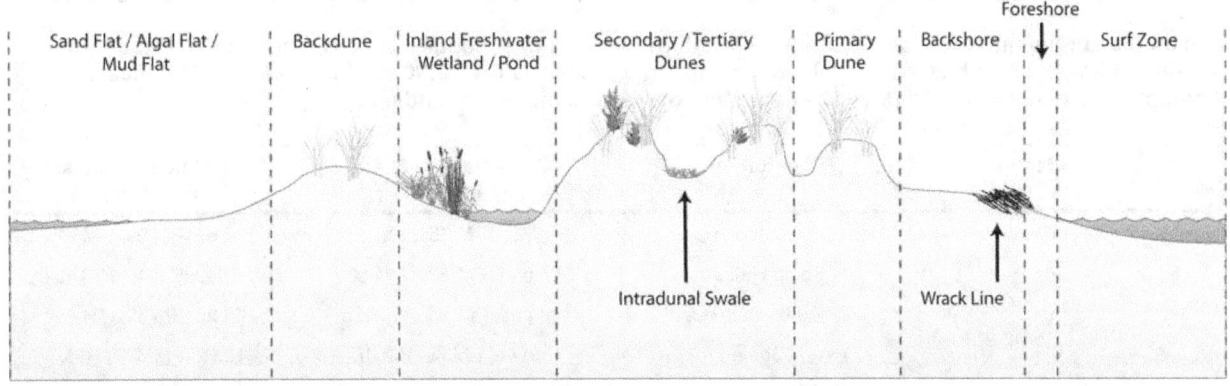

Figure 6. Conceptual diagram of shorebird habitat-type juxtaposition of at Cape Hatteras National Seashore.

A line transect (Anderson et al. 1979) was used to sample each sampling unit; however the high-intensity sites are spatially broad and one transect would not adequately cover the unit. These areas were systematically subdivided into roughly 300-m wide areas; each containing a transect to facilitate sub-sampling of these sampling units and ensure coverage of all habitat types within the high-intensity sites.

A combination of high- and low-intensity sites within a park subunit were sampled each day. Groupings of sampled sites and the order in which they were sampled were based on the methods presented in Byrne et al. (2009) to ensure a spatially balanced random sampling of both high- and low-intensity sites throughout the park. The sampling schedule was designed in alternating fixed daily intervals (e.g., Wednesday: high-intensity – 0700 – 1200, and low-intensity sites – 1300 – 1800, Thursday: low-intensity – 0700 – 1200, and high-intensity sites – 1300 – 1800) throughout the annual sampling event. This alternating procedure facilitated obtaining an approximately equal number of sampling events by tidal stage.

In the high-intensity sampling regime, the spits / points were sampled in their entirety during each sampling event (i.e., all transects contained therein). The observer began observations of the unit (oceanside, soundside, or interior) closest to the access point for the site to avoid observer influence on birds prior to measurement. In the low-intensity sampling regime, only the unit specified was sampled during the designated time. No sampling unit was sampled at an interval of less than four days to avoid any potential across-day observer influence on focal-shorebird presence and maintain independence of observations. The sampling regime was on a rotating schedule with an eleven-month duration. Table 2 outlines an example sampling schedule for high- and low-intensity units and was designed to be conducted on a five-day work week, beginning Wednesday of each week with Mondays and Tuesdays off. The sampling order of high- and low-intensity sampling units was randomly determined. The migratory component of this protocol was defined as July – October and February – May. The wintering component was defined as November – December. High- and low-intensity sites were sampled from July – May to capture both of these periods.

Table 2.
Example annual migratory and wintering shorebird monitoring schedule for sampling units at Cape Hatteras National Seashore. Shaded cells indicate sampling to occur before 12:00 and unshaded cells indicate sampling to occur after 13:00. [PM – Park Mile; o – Oceanside; s – soundside; I - interior].

Order	Park Sub-unit	High-intensity Sites (Park Mile)	Low Intensity Sites (Park Mile)
1	Ocracoke	PM 75o, PM 75s, PM 75i	PM 62, PM 69, PM 71
2	South Hatteras	PM 58o, PM 58s, PM 58i	PM 40, PM 46, PM 49
3	Middle Hatteras	PM 45e, PM 45i, PM 45s	PM 29, PM 39, PM 44
4	Bodie	PM 4o, PM 4s, PM 4i	PM 2, PM 3, PM 18
5	Ocracoke	PM 59o, PM 59s, PM 59i	PM 63, PM 64, PM 73
6	South Hatteras	PM 58o, PM 58s, PM 58i	PM 50, PM 51, PM 57
7	Middle Hatteras	PM 45e, PM 45i, PM 45s	PM 30, PM 32, PM 35
8	Bodie	PM 4o, PM 4s, PM 4i	PM 23, PM 25, PM 27
9	Ocracoke	PM 75o, PM 75s, PM 75i	PM 61, PM 65, PM 74
10	South Hatteras	PM 58o, PM 58s, PM 58i	PM 47, PM 52, PM 56
11	Middle Hatteras	PM 45e, PM 45i, PM 45s	PM 37, PM 38, PM 42
12	Bodie	PM 4o, PM 4s, PM 4i	PM 21, PM 22, PM 28
13	Ocracoke	PM 59o, PM 59s, PM 59i	PM 66, PM 70, PM 72
14	South Hatteras	PM 58o, PM 58s, PM 58i	PM 41, PM 48, PM 53
15	Middle Hatteras	PM 45e, PM 45i, PM 45s	PM 31, PM 33, PM 34
16	Bodie	PM 4o, PM 4s, PM 4i	PM 0, PM 20, PM 26
17	Ocracoke	PM 75o, PM 75s, PM 75i	PM 60, PM 67, PM 68
18	South Hatteras	PM 58o, PM 58s, PM 58i	PM 54, PM 55
19	Middle Hatteras	PM 45e, PM 45i, PM 45s	PM 36, PM 43
20	Bodie	PM 4o, PM 4s, PM 4i	PM 1, PM 19, PM 24

Field Methods

Field sampling was conducted following the methods in the SECN's wintering and migratory shorebird monitoring proposal (Byrne et al. 2009). The technique for quantifying focal-shorebird observations consisted of time-constrained transect-based surveys with distance sampling of all habitat types within each park mile (Anderson et al 1979, Buckland et al. 2001). Each transect was one-mile in length and was surveyed for 30 minutes. When a focal shorebird was observed, the habitat type in which it was observed, general activity (i.e., moving, flying, sedentary), and distance from the observer was recorded. The azimuth of the transect and azimuth to the focal shorebird was also recorded. Due to equipment issues, distance samples were only collected during the last four months of the study. General weather conditions, tidal stage, and potential sources of disturbance (i.e., vehicles, people, dogs) were also recorded within each sampling unit. The sampling units were also surveyed for beached shorebirds. When a beached or moribund shorebird was detected, the species, condition, and any obvious possible causes of death were recorded. Methods followed those developed by Byrne et al. (2009).

Data Analysis

Normalized counts (i.e., number of observations / unit of effort) were used for all calculations and most summaries, as a means to control for effort since effort varied across sampling units. Power analysis was conducted for piping plover, American oystercatcher, and red knot in accreted areas (i.e., high-intensity sampling units) and in accreted areas and beachfront areas combined (i.e., across sampling regimes). Our sampling objective was to secure 90% assurance (i.e., power) that we could detect an annual change of 20% in the mean of normalized counts (i.e., minimum detectable change) with a 5% chance of a false-change error (i.e., detecting a change when one does not actually exist). The power to detect annual and monthly trend was calculated with an equation for permanent plots without the finite population factor (Elzinga et al. 1998).

Detection frequency is a measure used to determine the relative likelihood of detecting a focal element in any given area. We used the number of groups of focal shorebirds encountered per transect rather than the number of individuals to avoid overestimation and a subsequent bias in our estimate. This measure was used as a tool to determine the timing of the wintering population of piping plover (i.e., when did detection frequency remain approximately constant) and was only calculated for piping plover because it was the species of greatest concern.

Abundance estimation is generally not possible for a migratory population of shorebirds except via multiple observers conducting simultaneous counts with distance sampling across the entire area of interest, as these populations are considered "open" even over short periods of time (i.e., the population exhibits one or more population processes during the sampling period – births, deaths, emigration, or immigration). A basic requirement of abundance estimation for any species using distance estimation is that the population is "closed" (i.e., the population of interest does not exhibit any of the aforementioned processes). Although abundance estimation may be possible for the wintering population of shorebird species, it is unlikely that an observer will collect the 80-100 statistically independent distance-to-bird measures necessary to calculate a valid detection function g(x) (Buckland et al. 2001), as the wintering population of many shorebird species is estimated to be small and detection frequencies are low.

The primary purpose of distance-to-bird sampling as part of this study was to calculate an effective strip width (i.e., the distance at which detection probability decreases significantly) and, subsequently, determine transect spacing to ensure all areas have an equal likelihood of being sampled and facilitate random-transect placement. The secondary purpose was to determine if 80-100 distance measures for each species could be collected and a wintering abundance estimate be calculated. Other purposes for the inclusion of distance sampling included were to a) determine if the shape criterion was met (i.e., detections are certain along the transect and remain certain for a given distance from the transect), and b) determine if detectability remains constant by species and by month. For example, if counts are equal over time period t_1 and time period t_2 but detectability differs between the two time periods, it is likely that any subsequent abundance estimate is incorrect and therefore not comparable. We used Program DISTANCE to analyze distance data (Buckland et al. 2001).

Pearson and Spearman correlations (Zar 1999) were conducted to assess relationships between tidal stage and habitat use, and habitat use and observed counts. Transformed or untransformed count data were not normally distributed; therefore a Mann-Whitney test was used to compare normalized counts in high intensity and low-intensity sites (Zar 1999).

Results

Piping Plover

The majority of piping plover observations occurred in mudflat/ algal flat and foreshore habitat types (Table 1, Figure 7). Observed use of mudflat/ algal flat habitat types was not related to tidal stage; however the majority of observations in the foreshore habitat type occurred at low tide. However, tidal stage was not significantly correlated with observed habitat-type use ($r_s = 0.21$). Detection frequency of piping plover was highly variable; however relative stability in this measure (i.e., $m = 0.02$) from mid-November to mid-February, under a constant sampling effort, provides some evidence of a closed population during this period (Figure 8). The fall migration appears to peak in August (Figure 8). The spring migration likely peaks in May, but nest initiation by piping plover and logistical issues precluded sampling later than April 2007. The three highest single-day counts (for sampled areas only) were 24 in July 2006, 50 in August 2006, and 14 in April 2007.

American Oystercatcher

The majority of American oystercatcher observations occurred in foreshore and mudflat/ algal flat habitat types (Figure 10). American oystercatcher appeared to use the foreshore habitat type during both tidal extremes; however mudflat/ algal flat appeared to be used exclusively during high tide. Tidal stage was not significantly correlated with observed habitat-type use, however ($r_s = 0.25$). The highest number of birds appear to occur in August and CAHA does not appear to have a wintering population of American oystercatcher (Figure 11). The two highest single-day counts were 13 in October 2006 and 12 in August 2006.

Red Knot

Red knot observations overwhelmingly occurred in the foreshore habitat type (Figure 12); with a relatively equal distribution of observations occurring at low and high tides. Tidal stage was not correlated with observed habitat-type use ($r_s = 0.27$). Monthly red knot counts were highly variable by month (Figure 13). Red knot detections are generally of large groups (ca. 100 birds) along beachfront areas. The two highest single-day counts were 230 in February 2007 and 170 in November 2006

Wilson's Plover

Only seven Wilson's plover observations were made during the entire sampling seasons. The authors do not attribute this to the absence of Wilson's plover at CAHA, but rather due to a realized difficulty in proper identification of this species by field personnel (i.e., insufficient training). All of the observations occurred in the foreshore habitat type during low tide.

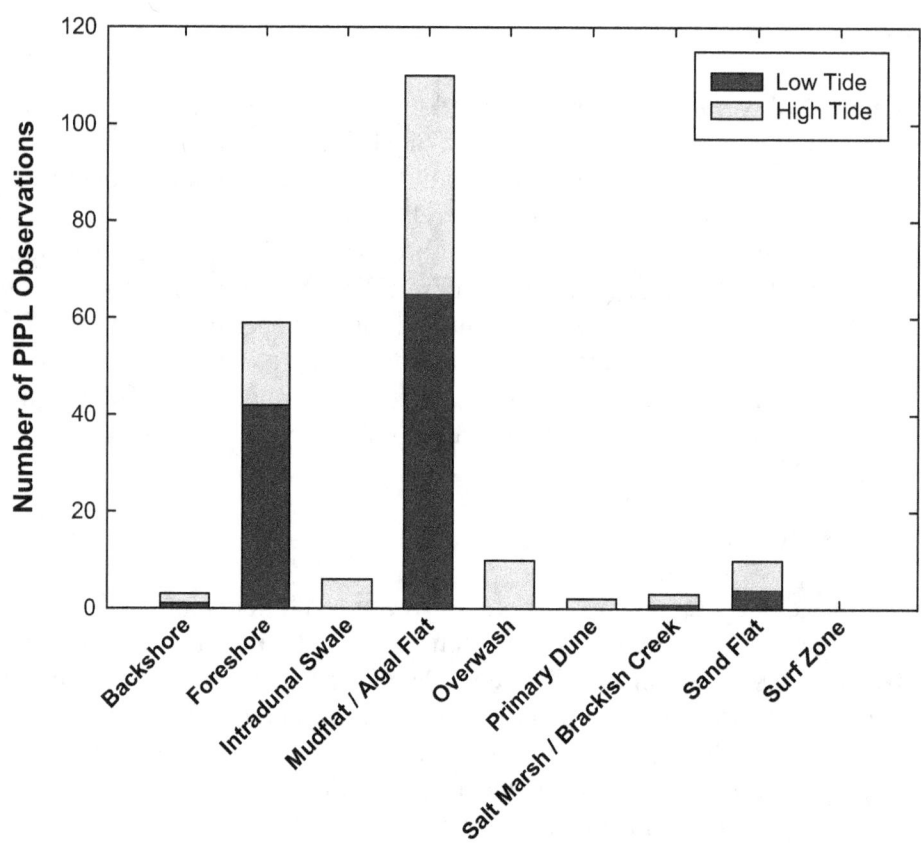

Figure 7. Number of piping plover (PIPL) observations by habitat type and tidal stage at Cape Hatteras National Seashore, 2006/2007.

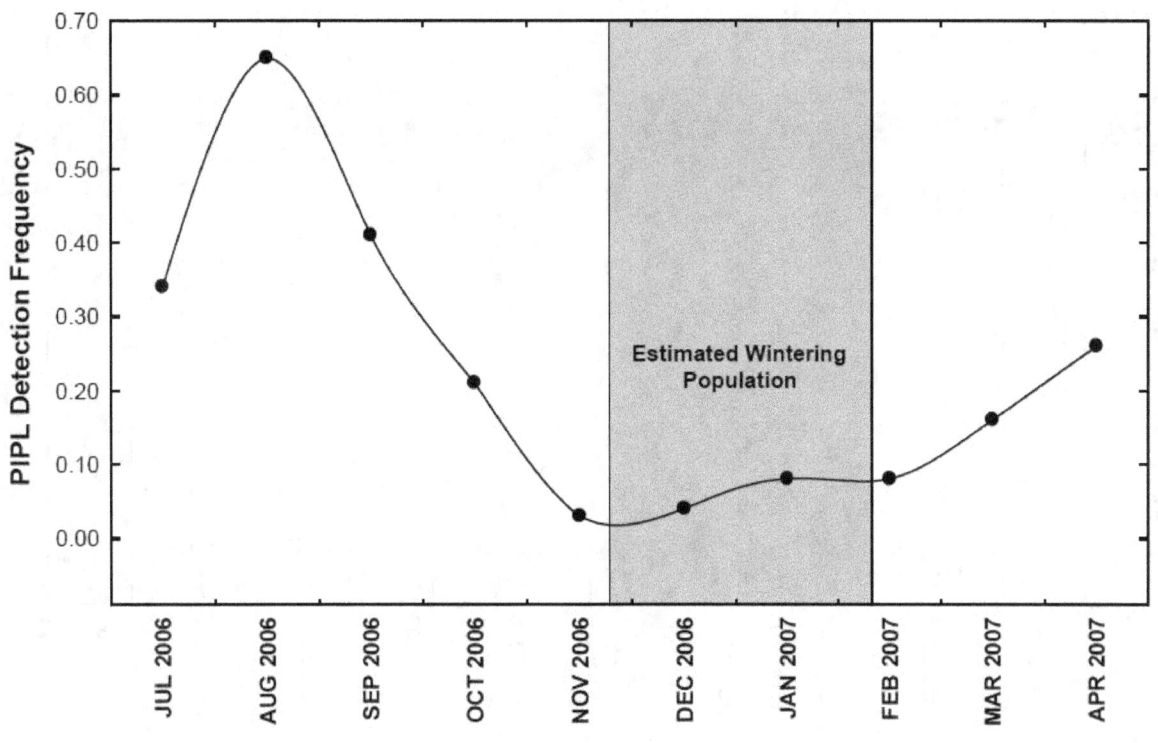

Figure 8. Detection frequency for piping plover in accreted areas at Cape Hatteras National Seashore, 2006/2007. Estimated wintering population shaded in gray.

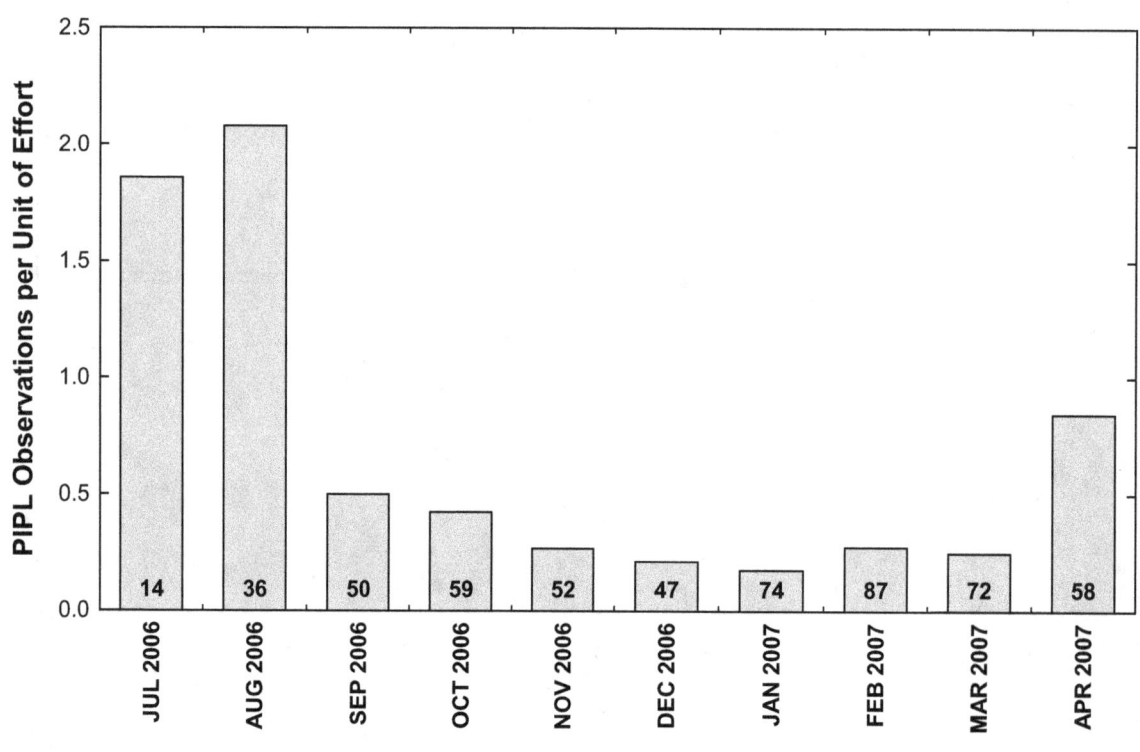

Figure 9. Monthly normalized counts of piping plover (PIPL) and number of sampling events at Cape Hatteras National Seashore, 2006/2007. Normalized counts are calculated as number of birds observed per 30-minute sampling event.

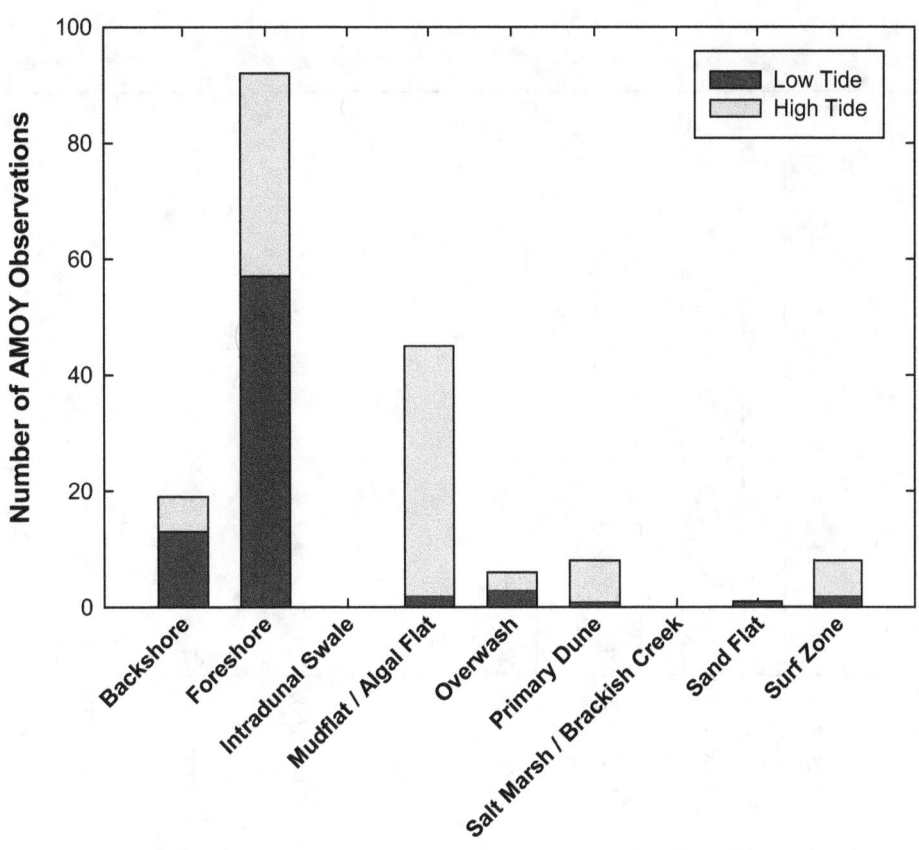

Figure 10. Number of American oystercatcher (AMOY) observations by habitat type and tidal stage at Cape Hatteras National Seashore, 2006/2007.

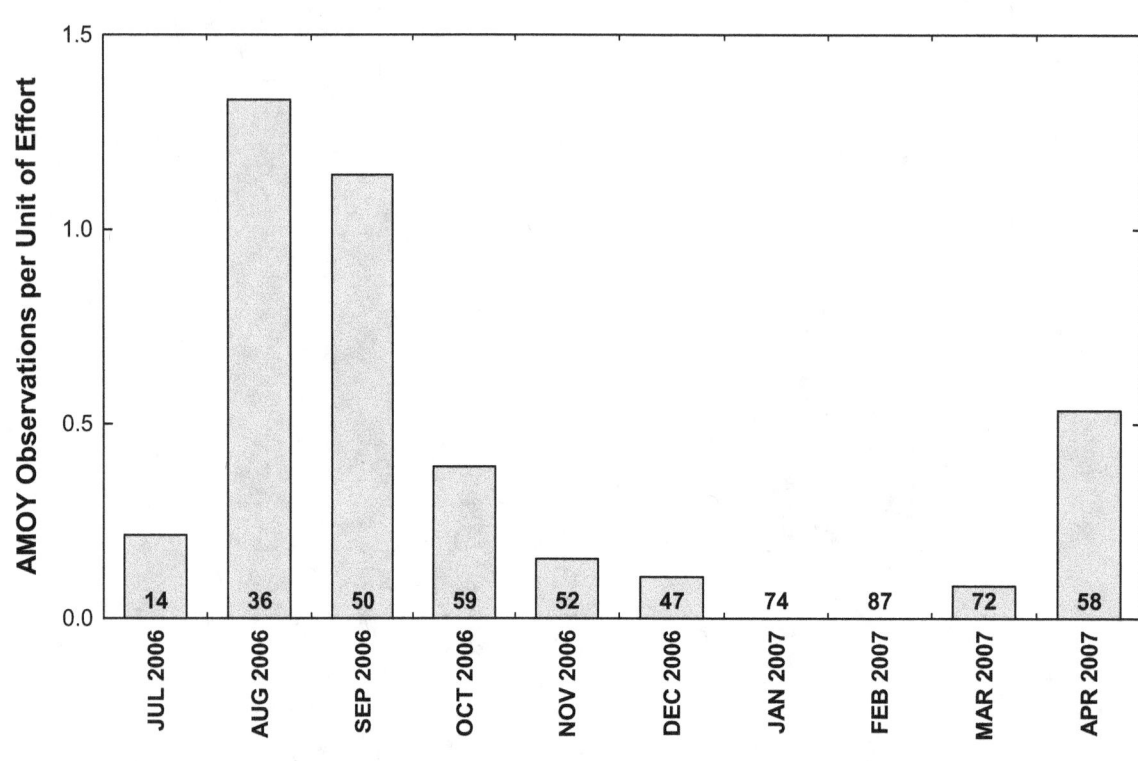

Figure 11. Monthly normalized counts of American oystercatcher (AMOY) and number of sampling events at Cape Hatteras National Seashore, 2006/2007. Normalized counts are calculated as number of birds observed per 30-minute sampling event.

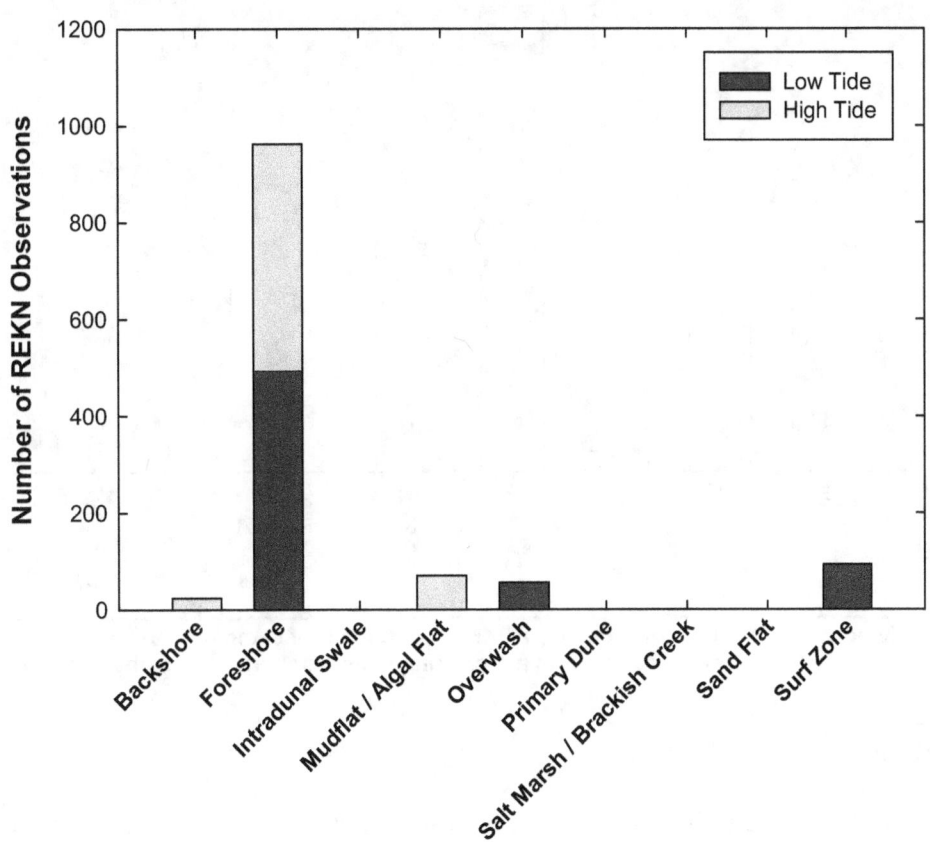

Figure 12. Number of red knot (REKN) observations by habitat type and tidal stage at Cape Hatteras National Seashore, 2006/2007.

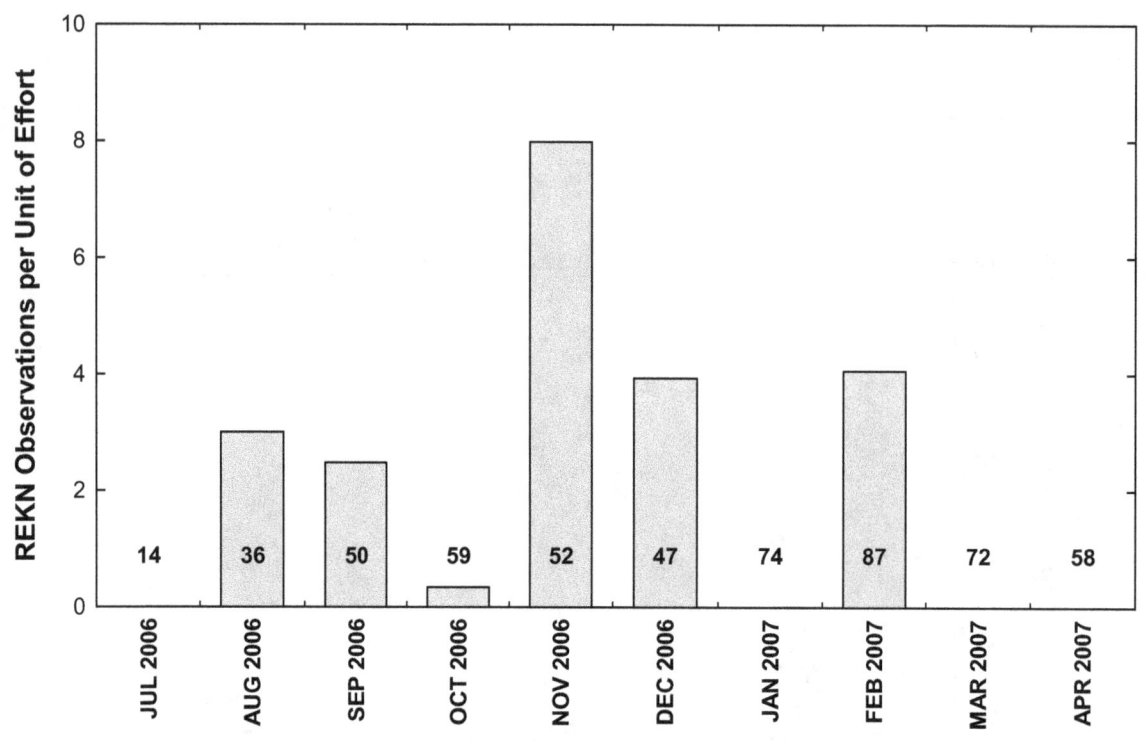

Figure 13. Monthly normalized counts of red knot (REKN) and number of sampling events at Cape Hatteras National Seashore, 2006/2007. Normalized counts are calculated as number of birds observed per 30-minute sampling event.

Power Analysis

As previously stated, our sampling objective was to secure 90% assurance (i.e., power) that we could detect an annual change of 20% in the mean of normalized counts (i.e., minimum detectable change) with a 5% chance of a false-change error (i.e., detecting a change when one does not actually exist).

In the accreted areas, we exceeded our desired power outlined in the sampling objective for annual normalized counts of piping plover and American oystercatcher (i.e., 99.4% and 82%, respectively). For red knot, however, we only achieved 64% power to detect a 20% change in annual normalized counts, but have 93.5% power to detect a 30% change. Sample size for sampling units in accreted areas was 279.

Park-wide (i.e., pooled values from accreted areas and beachfront areas), we did not meet our sampling objective for any of the three species. For piping plover, we only achieved 78.5% power to detect a 40% change, and 93.1% power to detect a 50% change. Only 40% changes in annual normalized counts for red knot can be detected (power = 92.5%), and 30% changes in counts of American oystercatcher (power = 93.4%). Park-wide sample size was 530.

Given our first year of data, we do not have power to detect monthly trends either park-wide or in accreted areas alone.

High Use Areas

Transformed or untransformed count data were not normally distributed, therefore a Mann-Whitney test (Zar 1999) was used to compare total normalized counts in accreted sampling units (i.e., those under the high-intensity sampling regime) and beachfront and other sampling units (i.e., those under the low-intensity sampling regime). Counts of piping plover were significantly higher in accreted areas than beachfront areas at the Park ($U = 339.0$, $n_1 = 57$, $n_2 = 6$, $p < 0.001$, two-tailed test). Red knot counts were also higher in accreted are than beachfront areas ($U = 302.0$, $n_1 = 57$, $n_2 = 6$, $p < 0.001$, two-tailed test). American oystercatcher counts, however, did not differ among accreted areas or beachfront areas ($U = 243.5$, $n_1 = 57$, $n_2 = 6$, $p = 0.09$); although suggestive of a difference that more birds occur in accreted areas than in beachfront areas.

Variability in normalized counts was very high for all three species, with the 95% confidence interval including zero for American oystercatcher and red knot in spits/ point sampling units (i.e., accreted areas) (Table 3)., and piping plover in non-spit sampling units (i.e., beachfront areas) (Table 4).

Table 3.
Normalized counts for American oystercatcher, piping plover, and red knot on spits/ point sampling units at Cape Hatteras National Seashore, 2006/2007.

Sampling Unit Description	American Oystercatcher	Piping Plover	Red Knot
Bodie Island Spit - Western Inlet	2.04	1.96	6.92
Bodie Island Spit - Central Oceanside	0.06	0.67	2.54
Cape Point	0.30	0.55	1.79
Hatteras Island Spit	0.57	0.14	0.14
Northeast Ocracoke Island	0.20	0.73	24.93
Ocracoke Island Spit	0.00	1.81	2.46
Mean	*0.53*	*0.98*	*6.46*
Standard Deviation	*0.77*	*0.73*	*9.32*
+/- 95% Confidence Interval	*0.61*	*0.59*	*7.46*

Table 4.
Normalized counts for American oystercatcher, piping plover, and red knot on non-spit / point sampling units at Cape Hatteras National Seashore, 2006/2007.

Sampling Unit Description	American Oystercatcher	Piping Plover	Red Knot
Park Mile 00	1.25		
Park Mile 01	0.60		
Park Mile 02	0.50		
Park Mile 03	2.60		
Park Mile 19			
Park Mile 20			
Park Mile 21			
Park Mile 22			
Park Mile 23			
Park Mile 24			
Park Mile 25			
Park Mile 26	0.80		
Park Mile 27	0.40		
Park Mile 28		0.25	
Park Mile 29			
Park Mile 30			
Park Mile 31	2.00		
Park Mile 32	0.75		0.25
Park Mile 33	2.00	0.25	
Park Mile 34			
Park Mile 35			
Park Mile 36			
Park Mile 37			
Park Mile 38			
Park Mile 39			
Park Mile 40			
Park Mile 41			
Park Mile 42			
Park Mile 43	0.29		
Park Mile 44	0.25		3.25
Park Mile 45			
Salt Pond	0.06	0 06	
Park Mile 47	2.33		

Sampling Unit Description	American Oystercatcher	Piping Plover	Red Knot
Park Mile 48		0.33	
Park Mile 49			15.67
Park Mile 50			
Park Mile 51			
Park Mile 52	1.00		
Park Mile 53	0.20		3.60
Park Mile 54			2.50
Park Mile 55			
Park Mile 56			
Park Mile 57	0.17		
Park Mile 59			
Park Mile 61			6.50
Park Mile 62			0.57
Park Mile 63			2.33
Park Mile 64			
Park Mile 65			18.33
Park Mile 66	0.50		
Park Mile 67			7.00
Park Mile 68			
Park Mile 69			2.33
Park Mile 70	0.60		
Park Mile 71	0.25		
Park Mile 72			2.67
Park Mile 73			
Mean	*0.29*	*0.02*	*1.14*
Standard Deviation	*0.61*	*0.06*	*3.40*
+/- 95% Confidence Interval	*0.16*	*0.02*	*0.88*

Additionally, approximately twice as many ORV's occur in the accreted areas compared to general beachfront areas. The highest number of normalized of ORV's occur during the fall months when migratory bird observations peak (Figure 14).

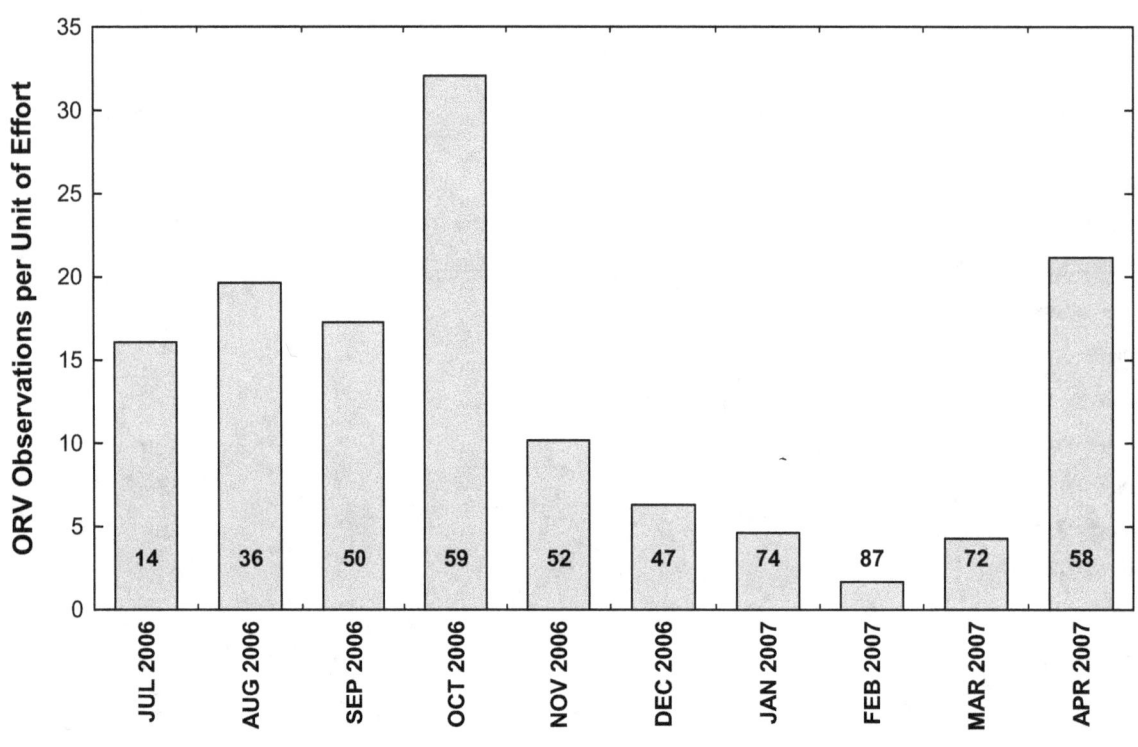

Figure 14. Monthly normalized counts of ORV observations and number of sampling events at Cape Hatteras National Seashore, 2006/2007. Normalized counts are calculated as number of vehicles observed per 30-minute sampling event.

Discussion

Habitat use patterns for piping plover identified as part of this effort are comparable to those identified by other studies (e.g., Haig and Oring 1985, Nicholls and Baldassarre 1990). These specific habitat types (i.e., moist substrate) play a vital role in shorebird survival during the migratory and wintering period. These habitat types are also important to red knot and American oystercatcher and many other shorebirds.

Our analysis indicates that piping plover and red knot occur more frequently in accreted areas at CAHA, and suggests that American oystercatcher do as well.

The lack of Wilson's plover data emphasizes the need for thorough training of field personnel to ensure proper identification and maximize sampling efforts.

Because of the observed substantial across- and within-site variability of piping plover observations, the general rarity of this species, and disproportionate distribution of habitat types across the park, a park-wide sampling design must include at least four times the sampling effort in the non-accreted areas to approximate 80% power to detect a 20% change in the number of birds observed park-wide. A detailed discussion of power as a function of sampling design is included in Byrne et al. (2009); the level of sampling in the protocol is adequate to support management decisions at the park, however.

Shorebird count data collected under this protocol results in a constant-proportion population index $E(C) = \beta N$, where $E(C)$ = the expected count, β = probability of detection, and N = the actual population size. The primary assumption of this index is that performance remains constant for varying values of N (i.e., it is linearly correlated), and this protocol is not designed to address this assumption or the efficacy of the index. As is frequently the case with population indices, difficulty exists in establishing the true relationship between index performance (i.e., validity) and true population abundance. Further implementation of the distance sampling component, however, will serve as a preliminary means to address the validity of the index by determining if detectability remains constant over time. For example, if the index reveals two counts that are substantially different at the same site between time year 1 and year 2 but detectability also varies between the two sampling events, it is more likely the differing counts reflect differences in detectability rather than differences in true population size.

Other potential ways to assess index validity are: 1) If the monitoring effort has moderate to good power (i.e., $\beta \leq 0.2$), this increases the confidence in index performance, 2) if distance sampling does result in a valid detection function and subsequent abundance estimate, the relationship between these two values can be explored, 3) the proportion of banded birds in a sample over time may also serve as a means to evaluate index validity (i.e., a mark/recapture – re-sight study); which can be done easily as part of this protocol, 4) implement a double-sampling approach (multiple observers) to estimate measurement error, or 5) since the wintering piping plover population assumed to be small, coordinated simultaneous counts repeated over several days would result in a timelier estimate with an associated confidence interval, however detectability will not be accounted for using this technique. It is important to note that inferences of abundance based on an index that has not been validated can result in incorrect conclusions and assumptions.

Management Implications

Based upon the results from the first year of monitoring data and discussions with CAHA staff, additional measures were added [e.g., whether birds were detected inside or outside closures; refer to Byrne et al. (2009) for details.

Strong evidence exists that piping plover use the accreted areas at CAHA more than general beachfront areas. These areas are also popular spots for ORV's. Based upon these observations, these areas have the highest likelihood of interactions between ORVs and piping plovers. Recreation-induced stress and the bioenergetic impact on shorebirds is very difficult to measure, although the impacts of persistent stress can be inferred from declining populations. More specifically, when combined with other shorebird stressors such as repeated flushing while foraging or from sheltered areas during inclement weather, stress can have a cumulative negative effect on fecundity and overwinter survival. A liberal approach to closure boundaries would be the most proactive strategy until future research quantifies the energetic expenditure related to different forms of anthropogenic stressors occurring in areas used by piping plovers and other shorebirds. This is of particular importance since CAHA plays an integral role in shorebird conservation by providing migrating and wintering habitat for many shorebirds species. Based on the findings in 2006-2007, the majority of piping plover observations occurred in foreshore and other moist-substrate habitat types within or adjacent to accreted areas; therefore closures in these identified high-use areas and habitat types should provide adequate access to both foreshore and other moist substrate habitat types (e.g., mud flats, sand flats, algal flats).

Literature Cited

Anderson, D.R., Laake, J.L., Crain, B.R., and Burnham, K.P. 1979. Guidelines for line transect sampling of biological populations. Journal of Wildlife Management 43:70-78.

Bloom, A. 1998. Geomorphology: A systematic analysis of late Cenozoic landforms, Third edition. Prentice Hall, Upper Saddle River, NJ, USA.

Buckland, S.T., D.R. Anderson, K.P. Burnham, J.L. Laake, D.L. Borchers, and L. Thomas. 2001. Introduction to distance sampling: estimating abundance of biological populations. Oxford University Press. 432 pp.

Brown, S.C. C. Hickey, B Harrington, and R. Gill. 2001. The U.S. Shorebird Conservation Plan. Manomet Center for Conservation Sciences, Manomet, MA, USA. 64 pages.

Byrne, M.W., J.M. Maxfield, and J.C. DeVivo. 2009. Migratory and wintering shorebird monitoring at Southeast Coast Network Parks. National Park Service, Fort Collins, Colorado.

Cohen, J.B. 2005. Management and protection protocols for the threatened piping plover (Charadrius melodus) on Cape Hatteras National Seashore, North Carolina. U.S. Geological Survey.

Cohen, J.B., S.M. Karpanty, D.H. Catlin, J.D. Fraser, and R.A. Fischer. 2008. Winter ecology of piping plovers at Oregon Inlet, North Carolina. Waterbirds 31: 472-479.

Daubenmire, R. 1968. Plant Communities: A Textbook of Plant Synecology. Harper and Row, New York, NY, USA. 300 pp.

Davis, M.B., T.R. Simons, M.J. Groom, J.L. Weaver, and J.R. Cordes. 2001. The breeding status of the American oystercatcher on the east coast of North America and breeding success in North Carolina. Waterbirds 24(2): 195-202.

Donaldson, G.M., C. Hyslop, R.I.G. Morrison, H.L. Dickson, and I. Davidson. 2000. Canadian shorebird conservation plan. Canadian Wildlife Service, Ottawa, Canada.

Elzinga, C.L., D.W. Salzer, and J.W. Willoughby. 1998. Measuring and monitoring plant populations. BLM Technical Reference 1730-1, Denver, CO, USA.

Erwin, R.M., C.J. Conway, S.W. Hadden, J.S. Hatfield, and S.M. Melvin. 2003. Waterbird monitoring protocol for Cape Cod National Seashore and other coastal parks, a protocol for the long-term coastal ecosystem monitoring program at Cape Cod National Seashore. Long-term Coastal Ecosystem Monitoring Program, Cape Cod National Seashore, Wellfleet, MA, USA.

Federal Register. 2008. Endangered and Threatened Wildlife and Plants; Revised Designation of Critical Habitat for the Wintering Population of the Piping Plover (*Charadrius melodus*) in

North Carolina; Final Rule. Federal Register 50 CFR, Part 17, pages 62815-62841.

Haig, S.M. and L.W. Oring. 1985. The distribution and status of the piping plover throughout the annual cycle. Journal of Field Ornithology. 56: 334–345.

Harrington, B.A., J.P. Meyers, and J.S Grear. 1989. Coastal refueling sites for global migrants. Pages 4293-4307 in Proceedings of the Sixth Symposium on Coastal and Ocean Management, O.T. Magoon, H. Converse, D. Miner, L.T. Tobin, and D. Clark, editors. American Society of Civil Engineers, Salem, MA, USA.

Harrington, B.A. 2001. Red knot (Calidris canutus). Pages 1-32 in A. Poole and F. Gill, editors. The Birds of North America. The Birds of North America, Inc., Philadelphia, PA, USA.

Hoffman, C. and W. Shroyer. 2004. Geomorphic mapping of Cape Hatteras National Seashore, Wright Brothers National Memorial, and Fort Raleigh National Historic Site, Overview of methods and deliverable (Draft). North Carolina Geological Survey, Raleigh, NC, USA.

Hoopes, E.M. 1994. Breeding ecology of piping plovers nesting at Cape Cod National Seashore. National Park Service, South Wellfleet, MA, USA.

Komar, P.D. 1998. Beach Processes and Sedimentation, Second edition. Prentice Hall, Upper Saddle Rive, NJ, USA.

Lafferty, K.D. 2001. Disturbance to wintering western snowy plovers. Biological Conservation 101: 315-325.

Leatherman, S. 1979. Barrier Islands: From the Gulf of St. Lawrence to the Gulf of Mexico. Academic Press, New York, NY, USA.

Loegering, J.P. 1992. Piping plover breeding biology, foraging ecology, and behavior on Assateague Island National Seashore, Maryland. Virginia Polytechnic Institute and State University, M.S. Thesis, Blacksburg, VA, USA.

Meyers, J.M. 2005. Management, monitoring, and protection protocols for American oystercatchers at Cape Hatteras National Seashore, North Carolina. U.S. Geological Survey, Patuxent Wildlife Research Center, Laurel, MD, USA.

Nicholls, J.L. and G.A. Baldassarre 1990. Habitat selection and interspecific associations of piping plovers wintering in the United States. Wilson Bulletin 102:581–590.

Nol, E., and R. C. Humphrey. 1994. American oystercatcher (Haematopus palliates). In A. Pool and F. Gill, editors. The Birds of North America, Number 82, Philadelphia, PA, USA.

Piersma, T. and A.J. Baker. 2000. Life history characteristics and the conservation of migratory shorebirds. Pages 105-124 in L. M. Gosling and W.J. Sutherland, editors. Behaviour and Conservation. Cambridge University Press, UK.

U.S. Fish and Wildlife Service. 1988. Great Lakes and northern Great Plains piping plover recovery plan. 160 pp.

U.S. Fish and Wildlife Service. 1996. Piping plover (Charadrius melodus), Atlantic Coast Population, Revised Recovery Plan. Hadley, Massachusetts. 258 pp.

U.S. Fish and Wildlife Service. 2003. Recovery Plan for the Great Lakes Piping Plover (Charadrius melodus), Ft. Snelling, MN 149 pp.

Zar, J.H. 1999. Biostatistical Analysis. Prentice Hall, Upper Saddle River, NJ, USA.

NPS D-240, March 2009

www.ingramcontent.com/pod-product-compliance
Lightning Source LLC
Chambersburg PA
CBHW080928290526
45795CB00007BA/2685